# Praise About the Author

"Self-Portrait is a beautifully honest and poignant account of what family members experience when a loved one suffers from addiction. Phyllis wrote it with a heart to help others. Readers will benefit from the very real life lessons she learned as they apply her wisdom to their own journeys."

**Thomas Otten**
Assistant Vice President for Avera Behavioral Health Services

"Phyllis Jorgenson shares the pain and burden of living with someone suffering from substance use disorder in a frank and honest way. She bravely opens up about the hardships she faced in her marriage to Glenn when he was actively using. But this is not a story of defeat to the monster of substance use disorder. This is a story of triumph over the disease and the blessings that follow when you don't give up on someone. Phyllis also stresses how the problem can overtake everyone around it, but that self-care is a must for the survival for loved ones and friends. Phyllis offers us hope that recovery can be found and maintained, and that families can be restored."

**Angela Kennecke**
Journalist (Angela's daughter Emily suffered from substance use disorder and died of an overdose at the age of 21)

"Many books inform, and some books are significant. Self-Portrait is both! Phyllis Jorgenson's authentic, relational journey and advice will have an immediate and lasting impact upon those who love addicts…and, hope for transformational change that will restore healthy and fulfilling lives."

**Dennis Hoffman**
President & CEO: Volunteers of America, Dakotas

"Phyllis Jorgenson tells in simple but powerful words what it was like to live with an addict and how she found a path to her own recovery as her spouse found his way out of the darkness. If someone you love is struggling with addiction or living with an addict, this book will help you understand that you are not alone and will show you that there is hope, help and a role model to follow."

**Terry Woster**
Freelance Writer and Co-Author of "It's Great to be Alive:
Understanding Addiction and Offering Hope"

# Self-Portrait
### Phyllis Jorgenson

# Self-Portrait
### Phyllis Jorgenson

Help And Hope When Your Loved
One Is Suffering From Addiction

Project Published in Collaboration with Avera Health

THRONE
PUBLISHING GROUP

Copyright © 2019 by Avera McKennan
Softcover ISBN: 978-1-949550-19-1
Ebook ISBN: 978-1-949550-20-7

All rights reserved. No part of this book may be reproduced or transmitted in any form or by any means, electronic or mechanical, including photocopying, recording or by any information storage and retrieval system, without permission in writing from the copyright owner. For information on distribution rights, royalties, derivative works or licensing opportunities on behalf of this content or work, please contact the publisher at the address below.

Printed in the United States of America.

Cover Design: Amy Gehling
Lead Writer: Angela Tewalt
Editor: Dirk Lammers

Although the author and publisher have made every effort to ensure that the information and advice in this book was correct and accurate at press time, the author and publisher do not assume and hereby disclaim any liability to any party for any loss, damage, or disruption caused from acting upon the information in this book or by errors or omissions, whether such errors or omissions result from negligence, accident, or any other cause.

Throne Publishing Group
2329 N Career Ave #215
Sioux Falls, SD 57107
ThronePG.com

# Table of Contents

*Introduction* . . . . . . . . . . . . . . . . . . . . . . . . *ix*

## Part I

1. About Painting and Life . . . . . . . . . . . . . . . . .3
2. Blank Canvas . . . . . . . . . . . . . . . . . . . . . . 13
3. The Picture Changing . . . . . . . . . . . . . . . . . 23
4. Unrecognizable Art . . . . . . . . . . . . . . . . . . 35

## Part II

5. Starting Over . . . . . . . . . . . . . . . . . . . . . . 51
6. Self-Portrait . . . . . . . . . . . . . . . . . . . . . . . 63
7. It's Great to be Alive . . . . . . . . . . . . . . . . . 73

*Resources* . . . . . . . . . . . . . . . . . . . . . . . . . *89*

# Introduction

I am Phyllis Jorgenson, and I made a choice.

I want to start there, because I believe I'm still here today because of choices I made for myself. Years ago, I endured more anguish than I could have ever foreseen for my life. There were days I didn't even think I could bear another moment, but I know now that God used it so that I could be here to tell you that I am the spouse of an alcoholic, and I made a decision to accept that truth and embrace it as a big part of my life. Choices have the power to alter perspectives for a lifetime.

From my personal experience, I learned that families of alcoholics instinctively stay in denial and avoid acceptance of how significantly the addiction is overturning their own lives. But in addiction, everybody is hurting. There is no logic, and acceptance of that is a good place to start.

My husband, Glenn, has been sober for many years now, and I am grateful for the opportunity to share my story so that others might also find acceptance, help, and peace. But I only do so by choosing to live one day at a time, even today—just like you will.

# Self-Portrait

After Glenn got sober, we helped to establish treatment centers in the South Dakota cities of Pierre, Rapid City, and Sioux Falls (with eight outreach offices) where I saw myself in the family members who visited. It was important to me that we implemented some sort of family program for people like you and me, the ones who watch our loved ones slip away. And as I talked with them, I saw myself in their pain, suffering, and mental anguish. They were either docile or angry, but almost everyone was tense, frustrated, abandoned, and desperate for answers. *Please, anything.* Yes, I had those cries, too.

We plead for answers, because we love them dearly. We care about them, their well-being, and their existence in our lives. Sometimes we care so deeply that we stop caring for ourselves, as if we don't even realize that we are suffering, too. Renowned recovery author and speaker Claudia Black once wrote that as the addict becomes more addicted to the substance, we become more addicted to the addict (*It Will Never Happen To Me!*, 1987). While their attention narrows completely onto using, we focus completely on their whereabouts, their actions, and anything we might do to intervene. This not only makes us insane, it leaves very little attention toward anything or anyone else, including ourselves.

I waited far too long to get help or to look after myself, but a better life for you and me only comes when

## Introduction

we choose to focus on ourselves and not them. Just like the alcoholic is entirely responsible for their recovery, we are responsible for rediscovering ourselves and feeling some kind of peace again. I could not force my spouse to change so I could live a better life. That was on me. It's hard enough to change ourselves, let alone someone else, but if we change, the other person cannot remain the same. That's hopeful.

With help, I was able to change me, and *you can change you*.

Families of the addicted can get really squirrelly, because we endure a kind of pain and experience far different from that of the addict. The alcoholic is somewhat anesthetized, but we are not. We see and remember everything, which means we end up absorbing more of the trauma and resentment. I remember one particular story shared during a family program at River Park. A woman was intending to divorce her alcoholic husband after he came home drunk one night and threw out all of their child's birthday party preparations from the refrigerator. But when she asked him about it during family program, he was completely floored and responded to her, "I would never do something like that!" He had absolutely no recollection of his actions, and when she realized this, it changed everything for her. She was able to separate her spouse from the addict he had become, trusting that was not who he wanted to be either. You can work through that separation here, too.

Not only do these raw memories take a long time to heal, these scenarios speak to the evasion that exists within families of addiction. Because the disease creates so much isolation as a means of survival, so much is left unsaid. The addict does not want to talk about their addiction, because they are already ashamed, lonely, in denial, guilty, remorseful, and fearful of repercussions. And the family member learns to capitulate, because they learn that expressing any hurt or anger only widens the reach toward their loved one, so the relationship merely exists as two ghosts in the night. There are lost words, abandoned discourse, and little civility between two people who otherwise love each other.

Even for me today, years removed from the isolation, it is still difficult to recount the memories aloud. Not only could it reignite those memories of past actions, I believe that deep pain bypasses the emotions, as if the brain knows that's The Thing that hurts too much. But I'm here anyway to give you the solace I desperately needed during those times our marriage was adrift. I hope to guide you toward healing, acceptance, and, perhaps eventually, forgiveness.

I want to spend time with you in this book to help you first see three things: ***You did not cause the addiction,***

## Introduction

*you cannot control the addiction, and you cannot cure the addiction.* So often, family members will be desperate for some understanding of how so much damage has been caused and what went wrong. But addiction is not caused by one factor, and it definitely is not caused by something you did or did not do. We once visited a school for a family program presentation, and after all the kids had left the room, there was one little girl still sitting in her seat. As I approached her, she asked me, "You mean it's not my fault?" I said to her with all my heart, "Oh, no. On your worst day, it's not your fault." I hope you hear that here.

I also want you to concede that you cannot change your loved one's life for them. Just as there is no singular cause of the addiction, there is no prescriptive cure. Watching the disease advance from the outside, we expect that our unhappiness or fear would be enough for our loved one to stop using, but no amount of pleading or reasoning will cure their addiction. And we must understand that developing an addiction is never a wish or a goal for anyone. If they had as much control as we ask of them, they would use it, but they do not. The weight is insurmountable for them, too, but it is not our responsibility to carry that burden. We can care for them and not give up, but just as we will not change until we are willing, the change we wish to see in them will not come until they are willing—and only then.

# Self-Portrait

Then, I want to divert your attention to help you see and focus on one thing most of all: Working on yourself. I want you to see yourself for perhaps the first time in a long time. You deserve that. We spend so much of our lives trying to change other people, but it's more important that we find out who *we* are and make the best of *ourselves*, because that is the person we have to live with all of our lives. You must take care of you.

I did not do much for myself while we were raising a family years ago, but I did eventually paint, and it has become such a joy for me today. I love the opportunity to capture the beauty of our world and preserve the loveliness of a moment. In time, I began to see how much painting reflected the pleasures and pains of life, and it has been very healing for me over the years. Are you ready to do something for you?

As I begin to share my story, I want to remind you that this was my experience. This is what I did, but that does not mean it is how all people should act or react. Addiction is so fragmented and alienating that whatever might work for one person might not work for the other. But I do believe there are enough common denominators among us that you can glean *something* you can use to create a better way of life. I am one person who made it through, and I believe you can, too.

# Introduction

You may feel at times as if you have little left. You may even be ready to give up. I remember, too, feeling confused, angry, or at wit's end, but all those emotions mean that you *do still feel something*, which means there is hope. Before you run away, stay here with me first, and let's try to take care of you to see what kind of impact that can have on your life. Loving an addict can be quiet suffering, but to suffer in that is a choice, and you are made for more. No matter how desolate the days may feel, you will *always* have a choice, and making the choice to survive is powerful.

*We rejoice in our sufferings, knowing that suffering produces endurance, and endurance produces character, and character produces hope, and hope does not put us to shame, because God's love has been poured into our hearts through the Holy Spirit who has been given to us.*
Romans 5:3–5

# Part I

# Chapter One
# About Painting and Life

Out of all the paintings I've created over the years, my favorite is called "Proving Up," because it's about my Norwegian family. My grandmother Louise and her siblings, Hilda and Gerhardt, moved to Jackson County, South Dakota, to "prove up," which was the term for homesteaders who spent several months or even years living on the land to prove their desire to work the land. As for my grandmother and her siblings, they filed on adjoining land near Stamford to increase their acreage.

Whenever I would ask her about that time, she didn't say too much. I don't think it was a very pleasant time, but she did speak of adventure. My grandmother and her sister would shoot rattlesnakes and skin them to

# Self-Portrait

send home back east toward Canton, South Dakota, and they would wash clothes for the railroad crews as they worked their way through the area. They hauled their water from a pond and would insulate their homes with sod bricks to keep warm in the winter. Louise later told us about rigging her mattress up on hinges so she could hang it on the wall to get some floor space in her tiny home. They had no choice but to be resourceful, and I imagine it was an interesting time.

The painting was inspired by a glass negative I found amid my grandmother's belongings, and it still speaks to me today. From a distance, the image is very romantic. We see adventure and feel admiration, curiosity, and wonderment. But when we take the time to really see and consider the context of the image, we can only begin to understand the courage, tenacity, endurance, creativity, bravery, and faith of the pioneers as they pursued their love of freedom amid the incredible vastness of the great prairie grasslands.

Life is like that, too—beautiful and romantic on the surface, but sustained only by all the courage and endurance underneath. It can take your breath away, if you let it.

Painting is something I had always wanted to try. I believe we are here on earth to create something better, and so I enjoy this creative process. I began painting when

## About Painting and Life

our two daughters were in high school. Glenn was sober and we both were working through our own programs. Painting was for me. Some gals and I got together once a week and started painting ceramics before we moved on to canvas. We would critique each other's work and just enjoyed having social time together with like-minded people. It was nice.

Just like my grandmother's homesteading years, there is both adventure and learning within the painting process. There is both pleasure and pain, but it's all worth it. There is always a definitive starting point, but it's difficult for me to know when it's done. I may have a plan when I start, but it will probably change, and that isn't always easy to accept. Even still, it's satisfying to be able to concentrate on one thing for a time and learn to work through the frustration and the joy. I'm able to put any thought or emotion I'm feeling into my paintings as if it's safe there, and I'm really drawn to that.

I believe anybody can paint if they so desire. It's a wonderful form of self-care that's an inexpensive investment and while painting was mine, I encourage you to find your own form of self-care. You just have to work at it and find the right tools. For painting, you need quality

## Self-Portrait

brushes and paints in many shades. Your paints cannot be too oily or too dry, and the nicer paints are much easier to move around the canvas. I like to work with oil paints, personally, because the colors are so rich and lend themselves to many revisions over a period of weeks or years. Revision is comforting, except that makes it more difficult to know when to quit. Someone once advised me to just leave it alone and watch my progress from one project to the next. I try.

You need many different sizes and heft of brushes, and you have to tend to them the way you would any type of tool. Each brush controls the size and shape of your strokes—a thicker brush to cover fast, a softer brush for finer lines. For every stroke, there is a different brush, and sometimes you'll need to sacrifice a brush by rough use. That's just the way it is. You could also use an easel to hold up your canvas at a comfortable height for working. You may not think it's necessary, but it supports the painting without interfering.

Other than tangible tools in painting, I need time, education, and a willingness to learn. Having a community around me encourages me and inspires me to always be learning something new—we all see things differently. When the gals and I painted together, we would all be working on the same image, but each painting looked different. Whether their strokes were looser or tighter,

## About Painting and Life

soft or stark, their perspectives were not at all the same, and I was always intrigued by that. It's so true that what you see depends on where you sit.

Working with an art teacher has taught me that professionals help fine-tune the process. My teacher always has an experience to share, so I have to listen carefully. And when I watch her work, the way she uses her brush and lays down the paint, it is such a learning experience for me, because she makes it look so effortless. But I know she struggles through it, too. We all do, at some point or another.

There is risk in painting, because once I am willing to start, any move or stroke may or may not work out, but it will always inform. And I still have to be willing to finish. Surely, I may have to set it aside for a time and move on to a new painting with what I learned from the previous effort, but eventually, I always return to the painting at a time when I am in a better place, mentally or emotionally, to see it through. All things materialize, however long it takes.

But none of this matters if I don't have a vision. The brushes and the paint and the teachers and the time—all of it is irrelevant if I don't have an emotional connection or attachment to the subject and a desire to paint. If I want to paint, I have to look beyond the canvas in front of me and yearn for the truth I'm seeking in the work.

# Self-Portrait

The bittersweet realization is that so much of my dear painting is like dealing with addiction—or any battle in life. Even in joy, we are never far from the sorrow. But just like I need to look beyond my canvas in front of me, in addiction, I need to look beyond the afflicted person. I need to have a vision of how life can be better, or I will never see the finished work. Hope encourages me to soldier on.

In an emotional situation, it is so difficult to see clearly what is actually going on around you. Denial and anger make it hard to clear your head and recognize the disease for what it is. But if you get a vision for how life *can be*, looking beyond the shadows and embracing the depth, you can fully exhale once again.

For Glenn and me, I envisioned a sane, positive, useful life for us, full of possibilities. I was stubborn and easily affected by my preconceived plans for our marriage. But once I gained perspective and took time to see our life for what it was, everything changed—not for the better or for the worse, but with the acceptance I needed in my heart to live a fulfilling life. For me.

Just like I need a willingness to take risks in my paintings, you must be willing to get help or you will not make any progress and the problem will only continue to reign. We simply are not as in control of our lives as we wish we could be. Yes, upsetting the applecart can be

## About Painting and Life

frightening, but if we desire our lives to be different, we must make an effort. You need tools here, too, like education and community to guide you and people to support you—"easels" to hold you steady without interfering in the work. It's all to aid in the tension and apprehension you will face. That exists in painting, too, as well as any other matter of the heart.

Choosing to seek help can be a fearful and emotional journey, but there is knowledge and experience out there that can absolutely provide hope along the way. If you listen and put in the work the way I did with my fellow painting friends, you will gain answers, perspective, and a better understanding that you are not as alone as you think. Because you are not, and you don't deserve to be going alone in this anyway. My prayers are with you.

Just like my paintings, I hope this lasts for a while and brings you the joy of a much better future. My self-portrait is nearly complete, and my hope now is that my own experience can encourage you as you cast your own vision for a changed life.

*The world is round, and so the place that may seem like the end may just be the beginning.*
Ivy Baker Priest

## Chapter Two
# Blank Canvas

I believe that God's original intention for humanity was for us to live for Him and bring others to Him. I believe He wants for us to live a productive life, do good, and then, just like parents, He wants us all home.

I believe God wants us to live with joy in His presence and with usefulness, obedience, and faith. I also believe that God wants us to live with peace—peace in us and peace amid others. "Finally, brothers and sisters, whatever is true, whatever is honorable, whatever is right, whatever is pure, whatever is lovely, whatever is admirable—if anything is excellent or praiseworthy—think on these things ... and the peace of God will be with you" (Philippians 4:8). This one verse has been such

# Self-Portrait

a life preserver for me. It helps me see the positive, which makes me grateful, and I have found that it is very hard to be unhappy when I am grateful.

If I were to paint a picture that would symbolize how God intended us to live, I think I would paint a happy, contented family, working together on something worthwhile in bright light. It would be very pleasant, and the colors would include yellow for sun and happiness, red for love and joy, green for life, and maybe even all the colors of a rainbow. The feeling would evoke joy, peace, and service, and it would set a mood that would draw in the viewer. I might even include nice foliage—fruit trees, vegetables, flowers, and monarchs.

I think all my paintings start this way, with a simple vision of peace, light, and joy, all inspired by the simplicity of vistas, trees, bluffs, people, or old buildings. I wonder what stories they could tell if they had a voice, and so I like for my paintings to capture a moment in time that brings along with it a memory to recapture over and over, like in "Proving Up"—which, by the way, is what we are doing here together.

As far as God's intention for marriage, I believe He desires two to become one, and that the couple be God-fearing, honoring, and supportive of one another. We often get married and then want to change that person

## Blank Canvas

into whatever it is we think we need or have in mind for a mate. But I believe that if we were to reach that goal, we'd say, "Well, this is not the person I married, and I don't think it's any better. I miss the challenge." We wouldn't be satisfied, and that's why God asks us to honor our partner's wishes, hopes, and desires. I think He also intended our unions to be a lot smoother than we make it—we are working on that still.

I think the elements of a good marriage include respect, appreciation, thoughtfulness, commitment, forgiveness, and a sense of humor. God uses marriage to help us mature and enrich our lives, which is why we need to tolerate the way they put the toilet tissue on, for example. It can be a point of contention, but is that really a hill on which to die?

Having these positive elements in a marriage produces security, harmony, and good company between two people. If there are children in the home, it impacts them tremendously because they, too, feel secure and grow up to be good citizens. All of this matters, because if any of these elements are lost, only then do you realize the significance of that relationship in your life. "Love is a harsh and dreadful thing to ask of us," Dorothy Day once wrote, but sometimes we need to decide to love in spite of what is happening. There were many times when our

# Self-Portrait

commitment was the only glue keeping us together. Love is so important.

When Glenn and I married, I didn't have too many expectations, just a desire to be together. I grew up as an only child, and I think I longed for companionship. My parents were extremely loving, and I knew without a doubt that my mom would have died for me. But when I was growing up and nobody had any money, both my parents were very busy on the farm and in the fields. I spent a lot of time alone.

When I was four years old, my dad surprised me with a puppy sitting on the porch, and I went on to spend my entire childhood with "Pooch" by my side. He was exceptional. You don't get much guff from your dog! I enjoyed Pooch's company so much that I don't think I ever felt lonely. But when I met Glenn, it was as if he had made real this closeness in my life that I didn't even know I was missing. With him, it didn't matter what was ahead, so long as he was by my side. More than feeling hopeful, he gave me a sense of fulfillment.

We first met in high school in Hayti, South Dakota, when I was a freshman and he was a senior. We had initiation, and I was attired in long underwear and overshoes, but you can imagine the seniors were enjoying it.

# Blank Canvas

Afterward in the evening, during a get-together in the gym, Glenn came over to me and offered me a ride home.

We dated all through my high school career. Glenn was very romantic, very sweet, and he loved to buy me nice things. One summer, he surprised me with a name-brand watch that I wore for years and years, and still have today. It must have taken a large share of his summer earnings! He was a very good basketball player, very persuasive and kind. We would go to movies together, to basketball games, or just drive around or watch people go by.

We married three days after I graduated from high school. I was 18 years old, wore heels, spent $5 on my wedding dress, and my mom baked the cake. For our honeymoon, we spent the first night in Sioux Falls, the second night in the Black Hills, then a third night in a cheap Rapid City motel before returning to Pierre, where Glenn was starting a job with the state. He always wanted to be successful, and I just wanted him to be happy.

My hopes regarding our life together were like that of many young wives, just wanting things to be good and wanting to do it all together. What more would we need, right? We felt very mature and ready for anything and everything. I had always wanted to be a mother, and I knew he would be a good provider. I had dreams of beauty, love, and walking hand-in-hand down the rose-petaled road of life.

# Self-Portrait

The beginnings of our marriage were like that of a blank canvas. When I first begin a painting, it's important that I am prepared. I must have an idea and vision in mind, and I must have all equipment near me so as not to be distracted. I like to be comfortable, sitting in good posture and in a quiet environment, but not outside where there might be bugs or noise. If I am not ready, I might set myself up for failure or easily lose sight of the vision. But my art teacher tells me that I think too much and just need to do it, so I try still today.

In life, we tend to float around, distracted, bothered, or afraid, but if we don't stay in motion we will never see the finished work. If I were to continue to belabor a painting and not just do the work, well, I'd never be satisfied. So if I prepare, believe in myself, and keep going, I will be more apt to take on the challenges, even if things don't go as planned.

I grow frustrated if a painting begins to divert from my original idea, so much that I can lose my zest and even give up. Sometimes, I have a certain area in a painting that I fall in love with, but as I go on, it becomes clear to me that it's actually the wrong thing in the wrong place or it distracts from the subject. If the original idea is no longer working, it's easy to lament on the difficulty of adjusting to change as opposed to adapting. For me, change is more difficult than fulfilling desires and

## Blank Canvas

following a plan, so I hesitate. Sometimes, I change, too, which causes my emotional connection to shift in some ways. That also can be frustrating. Change is quite hard, but expectations change, plans change, and perspectives change, too. In time, everything changes, whether or not we are prepared for the upheaval.

Amid the nearly two decades of Glenn's drinking, we lost some of the beauty. We weren't hand-in-hand anymore or didn't agree on things as much as I'd hoped, and trust was lost for a time. It wasn't very secure for a long stretch, and there were days I couldn't see an end in sight. There was no vision, and there was not much togetherness or hope.

Our blank canvas quickly went from a vision of beauty and love to that of betrayal and confusion. Not only did I not have any idea how to react or what to do, I didn't even know what alcoholism was or what to look for. I knew I had a neighbor growing up who was a drunk. He used to have liquor bottles everywhere in the weeds, just scattered all over the farmstead. He was clearly hiding it from someone, but you were a social pariah if you were an alcoholic, which meant the only ones I ever knew or saw were lying in the gutter. They surely weren't my husband. I just knew his behavior wasn't right. We were young and naive, and maybe that's what saved me from a lot of the early trauma. I never even saw the addiction coming.

*I can do all things through Christ
who strengthens me.*
Philippians 4:13

## Chapter Three
# The Picture Changing

Glenn never drank around me, and I never smelled alcohol on him. I did notice that right before we got married, he had changed a little, and, yes, it was a little concerning, but I never considered it to be drinking. It was just a gradual, uneasy feeling of how things were going.

Addiction is so sneaky—an evil thing that creeps up slowly into the home and even more slowly into acceptance. Social drinking is widely accepted, of course, and that's fine for some people. But for others, like Glenn, it just takes them down. And so down we both went.

Happy hour and socializing mattered to his job, and he liked to go to the bar after work. Most of the guys were there enjoying their beers, and because I was never

# Self-Portrait

around that when I was growing up, I just thought that's what successful people did. It was part of climbing the ladder, I suppose, and I didn't want to take it to mean a big deal.

But, gradually, the time he spent at home diminished, and he didn't invite me along when he'd go out with friends to drink. I was told by some of our friends that I was the "party pooper" of the group, never giving in to the peer pressure that certainly exists in adulthood as well, and that gave Glenn even more reason to exclude me. He would go to the bar right after work, and I'd be home fixing something to eat, wondering why he wasn't home. My dad was always home on the farm, so that was difficult for me to get used to—not having Glenn around as much as my dad. I didn't particularly like the way that made me feel, but I also thought it was the thing he needed to do for his work. And so it was.

Glenn had terrible headaches. The migraines started when he was a teenager and became more frequent as he got older. We see those same headaches in our family today. And so when the odd behavior and mood changes started, I blamed the headaches. It seemed obvious. I didn't know anything about alcoholism, but I knew he needed something for his pain, and we were always looking for ways to help him. Sometimes I thought maybe I did something in the home—cooking smells or perfumes—that caused his headaches. I was doing anything I could to take his pain away.

At one point, his headaches were becoming so unbearable that he would go to the hospital, often in the night, to get a shot of Demerol. The hospital was three blocks away from our house, so I would drive him over there, leaving our girls at home asleep in their beds. Even though it wasn't long, it hurt me very much to leave them alone. But when I came to the conclusion that he was more apt to get headaches when he was drinking, I told him I wouldn't take him to the hospital anymore. Even still, I did as much as I could to try and help the headaches. I didn't want him to be in pain.

I'm not an anxious person, but I would get concerned for him when he was gone more and more. *Was he in an accident? Where was he? Was he safe?* These thoughts consumed me in such an unhealthy way. In time, that fear turned to anger about his thoughtless deeds or embarrassing events. Glenn was in no way ever a cruel drunk, but he was certainly thoughtless and gone a lot.

Somewhere along the line, I would call the bar to see if he was there, and, of course, they always said he wasn't even though I was almost sure he was. A few times I'd even drive by to see his car parked in the front. I guess they wanted their paying customer more than my peace of mind.

# Self-Portrait

At times, it felt like everyone was on his side. Even the pharmacist at the drug store was quick to refill his headache prescriptions, whereas a friend had a tough time getting hers from the same pharmacist. In the later years, he even had a small accident on his way home one night, and the policeman just told him to go on home. Who was on my side?

For a long time, I didn't talk about Glenn's drinking. My friends didn't bring up the topic, so I wouldn't either. I didn't want to be the one who had a problem, and I thought it would just turn into *more* of a problem if I talked about it. So I didn't. It's not as if I felt alone, I just knew drinking too much wasn't something people should do, so I didn't want anybody to know that was my husband. In retrospect, I wish I reached out for help earlier than I did. We didn't have the resources that are available today and are listed in the back of the book. If you feel you need help, call someone who can help.

The first time I did try to talk to someone, I reached out to our pastor for support. His only reply was that I should "take a little more responsibility." He didn't know—nor did I tell him—that I already was taking on all the responsibility I could manage. But he didn't know anything about alcoholism either. So after having no success with the pastor, I just decided it was up to me. Marriage was very important to me, and if I wanted

## The Picture Changing

to keep our marriage going and allow our kids to have their father, I had to find my own way through this. I was stubborn, too, but I'm telling you that alone was not the way to go.

※ ※ ※

The reason I even reached out to our pastor in the first place was because of a call I received from our neighbor. At that point, I did not—or maybe chose not—to recognize Glenn's drinking for what it was, but when he called, he said, "I think Glenn has a drinking problem." I said, "We've got problems, but that's not it," and I just blew it off. But then it started me thinking, *Oh*, maybe he was right. He was a recovering alcoholic himself, and he might've even offered to help me, but I was too bowled over by the thought.

During this time of revelation, Glenn was spiraling. He would go on trips and not return on the day he planned. He and his best friend would go to Las Vegas for a few days and just forget to tell anybody. One time, his car was parked close to the airport, and I didn't even know he had left town. There was just this empty car in the parking lot, and I had no idea where he was. Soon that became normal, me never knowing when he'd be back home.

# Self-Portrait

One time, after he had returned from a trip, I opened our front door to find his suitcases on the porch. He had flown home, had the cab driver drop off his suitcases before taking him to the bar. That embarrassed me. I couldn't get them inside the house fast enough. It was hurtful, yes, but when anyone is addicted, they are in love with only one thing. Next to alcohol and prescription drugs, I was second in Glenn's life, and his compulsion to use was far bigger than his love for me or any promises he tried to make. For anyone, that hurts.

It was hard to identify and recognize the early signs at the time, because I didn't see them for what they were—I was always thinking instead of his painful headaches. I didn't know what the signs meant, and they confused me. Then when the more obvious signs surfaced, maybe I didn't even want to see them or I procrastinated. That could be denial, but it's in my nature to let things go for a while, and I was too busy anyway. Looking back, I was in quite a fog, just trying to keep going day by day—getting the kids to school, going to work, managing the home and the lawn and the kids on my own. I was just *existing*, hoping, and praying it would all go away and get better soon. I truly had no idea what I was doing. I was just hurting and exhausted.

I also felt rejected and abandoned. Why would he sabotage our marriage and time together like this?

## The Picture Changing

It didn't make sense to me, and I had no knowledge or idea of where to even start.

I didn't have conversations with Glenn about this, for many reasons. There was so much isolation between us. We had both grown up in strong Norwegian households in which people didn't talk about things. If they did, they surely didn't do it around the kids. It wasn't modeled that you ironed things out, and I believe that still exists today. I do remember one Christmas, however, when my folks confronted me. They came over to celebrate the holidays with us, but it was late, after our church Christmas service and after dinner, and by that time, Glenn had been drinking for a long while. Before they left, they said to me, "If he's still like this, we're not coming back next Christmas." I didn't even have to say anything. They knew things weren't good.

One time, I did muster up the courage to address Glenn's behavior. It bothered me that even if he was around, he was never fully present—just in this haze so that I'd rather he not even be in the room anyway. But attempting to have that useless conversation annoyed me to the point that I took his glass out of his hands and I threw it on the floor. It made a lot of noise, and then I had to clean it up. The rationale along the way was, I'll just have to clean it up myself anyway, so why bother? Another time, I remember him returning home sloppy

## Self-Portrait

drunk and swaying as he headed for the next room. As he passed the upstairs stairway, I had just reached a point of total frustration and I gave him a good shove, and he landed sitting on a stair. It was the only physical attack either of us ever made, but perhaps you can relate to simply just having enough. This was a breaking point for me.

The only other time I tried to confront Glenn, he shut me out. I remember thinking to myself, *We need to straighten things out*, so I approached him, but his only response? "I just shouldn't be married."

I knew right then that he didn't mean it and this was his defense mechanism. I think addicted people or even guilty people will use any weapon to *not* face the truth. They are embarrassed and ashamed, so they deflect the situation. Knowing this didn't make it less offensive, of course—I still took his hurtful comments personally—and it was especially frustrating that I was never able to get anywhere in those conversations. Glenn and I never reached a satisfactory solution or amends, but I had enough common sense to know he didn't *want* to be spiteful. Nonetheless, that didn't make me any less aggravated, disappointed, confounded, hamstrung, baffled, or defeated. I felt every single one of those things for a long time.

As the disease consumed my worries and thoughts, it also took over him. And if I wanted our marriage to

## The Picture Changing

stay intact, I had to be the one who hung in there. I went into this for life, but it was feeling more like a "life sentence." I could only see two choices: It either goes this way, or it doesn't go at all. I chose to stay, and I knew that if at least one person was working on the marriage, we still had a chance. If neither party participated, then our marriage couldn't work. So I worked, doing my best to remain practical, non-confrontational, and patient.

I remember so many long days as a child, when Mom and Dad would be working in the fields. While I waited for them, I'd be on my own, just sitting by the car and playing with the dolls and Pooch. I spent a lot of time under the sun, studying flies as they walked on my arm, waiting to see how long it would take them to bite. You learn to be patient in that, so I was. Maybe too patient? I waited far too long to get help.

*You cannot run away from a problem. You must at some time fight it out or perish. And if that be so, why not now, and where you stand?*

Robert Louis Stevenson

# Chapter Four
## Unrecognizable Art

I see addiction like the boiling frog in the kettle. When Glenn began to drink, both he and I were put into tepid water that was brought to a boil ever so slowly, so much so that we simply could not have perceived the danger ahead. Each new day was only a little bit worse than the day before, and it continued for years to creep up on us.

I believe this slow boil is why I had time for doubt, guilt, or confusion. Early on, I never even considered alcoholism, let alone urging Glenn into treatment. Other days, when I was sure there was a problem, I would still discern it to be smaller than it really was, because time moved differently. Days were slow and foggy, motivated merely by desperation to just get by. This was not

## Self-Portrait

a sensible state for knowing how or when to jump out of the boiling water.

But I was feeling the heat. A few years into our marriage, Glenn had started a restaurant in Pierre. We were in no shape to financially open a business, so I was vehemently against this idea, and I was not helpful. My staying out of the business was my protest against opening the doors in the first place, but the restaurant opened anyway, and there was a hostess. She moved from Sioux Falls to work at the restaurant, and she and Glenn had an affair. The timing was particularly bad, because she and I even got pregnant at the same time. I delivered my firstborn daughter in February, and she delivered her baby girl in March. We have a good relationship with Glenn's daughter today, but then, it was the most difficult, devastating, and tumultuous time of my life.

At this time, Glenn was drinking heavily, taking multiple prescription drugs every day, and not thinking clearly, if at all. Years later, he didn't even recall telling me about the affair, instead harboring a dark secret for years over something I already knew! He was truly in bad shape. But at the time he did first tell me about the other woman and her pregnancy, he suggested divorcing me because he felt obliged to leave me and take care of her. I was stunned, but I remember saying, "And that's the thanks I get?" My feelings were all over the map, none of them positive. I did insist that we not talk about divorce for at least a year, during which time he moved to California to seek help and therapy from a psychiatrist there.

I appreciated his desire to seek help, but not only did he leave me grieving an affair, he left me with our new baby, Jen. To be fair, our daughter was a gift. Even though I was suffering, she was there with me, beautiful and perfect, and I loved being a mother. I can't understand it, but I was filled with joy with this beautiful baby. Everything else fell away, and I rejoiced at her birth. She didn't save me—I had to save me—but she was the light of my life.

After "the news" of the affair, and before our daughter was born, Glenn and I had bought a house. (That should have been a sign that our minds weren't thinking very clearly!) But then, when he left for California, I decided to rent out part of the house to make some money. So for the first year of Jen's life, we lived upstairs, just the two of us.

Because it was just me trying to keep the house going, I had to get a job, and that was very difficult for me. It still hurts me today. My mom was always home when I was a child. I always thought I would be, too. I dreamed of staying home with our children and raising them, but when Glenn left, I didn't have a choice. Money was tight. I would only put a quarter tank of gas in the

## Self-Portrait

car every week, and I would make sure to have enough money for groceries, but I had to skimp on everything else so I could pay bills. I didn't miss work and didn't cause trouble, because Jen and I needed that money. Our bank account had been hemorrhaging for a long time. It felt as though there was a hole in the bottom, and the more I put in, the more that leaked out.

In some ways, it was easier. With Glenn gone, I didn't have to worry about where he was or what he was doing. Instead, I was plugging away at bills and housework, and I was sort of in control. It was somewhat of a silver lining, but it was still very much a tense, trying, desperate time.

I remember every morning walking down the stairway with Jen in my arms, leaving the house to take her to the babysitter, and there was always one step that would squeak. I would try so hard to be quiet and not wake the renters downstairs, but it squeaked nonetheless, and … Jen and I shouldn't have been walking down those stairs in the first place. We were supposed to be home together. That was the plan.

Needing people to rent our home and a babysitter and a job not to miss, that wasn't part of the plan. Betrayal and rejection and anger, that wasn't part of the plan. Glenn and I were to be happily married, enjoying our first baby—together—and none of it was coming into

## Unrecognizable Art

place. I remember feeling so out of control, fixating only on what I could do to get through the day. I was numb, tired, lonely, and sad, my own life detached from any romantic dream I once put in place.

A year after Jen's birth, Glenn returned home from California, a stranger to his own daughter. I knew I should forgive him, for my own mental health and the good of our family, and he really did seem to work on things for a while. We even welcomed our second daughter, Julie. Glenn was always a very caring and kind person, and often, I would see the man I loved. We would have picnics in the backyard, he would play with the girls and read them stories. I saw him there, lovingly in our home, but the drunken stupors eventually returned, taking me into a deeper spiral I could barely manage.

I don't think I myself even realized how far down this addiction had taken me, until I delivered a stillborn baby and my largest feeling was relief. It was devastating, but I don't think I could've handled three kids as well as Glenn. For someone who always wanted to be a mother to shift to thinking that the responsibility of another child would be too big a burden to bear, that was the boil rolling over. I knew it might be time to jump but I wasn't there yet.

# Self-Portrait

When I was at work, I spent a lot of time in the bathroom stalls, praying. I'm not sure whether I was praying for Glenn to get better or if I was just praying to get through the day, but I was absolutely relying on God. He was my only rock.

I would recite to myself over and over Philippians 4:8, "… think on these things, think on these things …" and I would trust God's promise that all things worked together for good. I was losing my sanity, but I was lucid enough to know that God was always there for me no matter what, and that I could talk to Him and even listen to Him if I was willing.

As I pleaded to God to get through each day, my priority was to take care of the kids. I prayed for the gumption and wisdom to do what I needed to do to keep a roof over their heads. But there was once a prayer to finish it.

One night, I cried to God in my sorrow, "I know that Glenn is in a position to get in an accident on the road. And if so, I'd like it to be final, because I don't think I want to take care of him in a wheelchair or worse. So, if that does happen, please, God, just finish it."

It is truly horrible to wish somebody were dead, but I just needed it all to go away. The desperation was palpable. I loved Glenn with all my heart, but I was praying to God to take him from this earth if it meant relieving

## Unrecognizable Art

me of my pain. Instead, God offered me resiliency and strength in the storm, and my faith got me through.

I don't believe it's possible to go through what I went through alone. You have to go somewhere and seek something or someone to withstand the adversity. I clung to God. I also believe that you have to work on yourself and get into better mental and physical shape so you can think clearly. At times, my thoughts were unmanageable—muddled, chaotic, and dark—but I couldn't use that. I needed a clear mind to save myself and our marriage. The addict is surely not thinking at all. At least we as the family have the luxury of a slightly more clear head. We must bring ourselves to a better place so we can regain our sanity and think healthy thoughts. And I know it's a valiant effort! We are so sad and tired of the injustice, but there is hope. You deserve to feel sane again. You deserve to focus on you in a healthy way.

# Part I

# Reflections

Addiction is a family disease. It does not just affect the afflicted. It affects those who love the addict as well, including spouses, children, parents, friends, and anyone who cares for the addict. There is a grave importance here to be as proactive as you can as soon as you can while continuing to support yourself, and then your loved one.

When you notice your loved one changing, you may feel as if you have done something to cause this behavior. But their disease is not your fault. Yes, every addicted person has to do something to deflect their actions, and that is likely on you, but rise above the guilt and take action by educating yourself as soon as you see early warning signs. These include physical

# Self-Portrait

clues, such as a change in eating or sleeping habits; emotional clues, such as a lack of motivation or moodiness; behavioral or relationship changes; and unexplained loss of money. If there are problems that come about due to chemical substances, then you are very likely looking at a dependency. Ignoring these signs could only enable further use, while early detection could save their life.

Addiction is a comprehensive disease that develops in the brain and touches every level of an addict's life. It is not based on weakness, lack of willpower, character flaws, or the fallacy that someone is a "bad person." At one point in their life, the addict may turn to alcohol or substances to cope with something and find that it is a stress reliever. Although the initial decision to use might be voluntary, changes occur in the brain over time that challenge an addicted person's self-control and hamper the ability to resist intense impulses to use. It has nothing to do with something a family member did or did not do, and it is important for you to separate that in your mind.

There are many parallel processes to be aware of as chemical dependency intensifies. For example, while the addict becomes more preoccupied with the drug, you become more occupied with the addict, consumed with thoughts of their behavior. You will also sense denial. The addict does not want to believe that the addiction is happening, and the family member does not want to believe that anything is happening to their loved one. Above all is a troubling tolerance. As the addict continues to

# Reflections

*build tolerance to the substance, you will notice that you are building a tolerance for your loved one's behaviors. In perhaps a way to cope, you accept hurtful comments or poor decisions, hoping it will all end soon, but you can regain some control of the situation by practicing continued awareness of these parallels as well as educating yourself and seeking support.*

*Despite any tolerance, a control factor may be prevalent in the home. It's instinctive to want to throw out the drugs or alcohol, to limit their access, to threaten them or try to "fix" their behaviors. But you cannot change an addict. They must want to change for themselves. You can, however, care about the addict and ask them what they need for support. And you can continue to educate yourself through community recovery support systems. Take care of yourself during this emotional time, find whatever it is you need for strength, and do not do this alone. Isolation only feeds the pain and weakens the courage you need to see this through. But you can see this through.*

# Part II

## Chapter Five
# Starting Over

It was winter when Glenn began his recovery. The girls were ages 11 and 13, and I was done. He had been managing a nice hotel and bar with a friend at the time, but his friend fired him. He, too, was done. I remember the friend coming to the house one day, so sympathetic and saying to me, "I'm going to have to fire Glenn. I can't have him there anymore." Of course, I knew that agony. My response was, "Do what you need to do."

Glenn's response to losing his job that night was to retreat to one of the vacant hotel rooms and drink himself to oblivion, and that's where I declared my own intervention. His friend told me where he was, I went to the hotel, found him in his room half coherent and simply told him that we loved him, but he had to do something.

# Self-Portrait

If he didn't, the girls and I were gone. Then I closed the door, went home, and finished the laundry.

In that moment, I didn't even consider whether he was going to listen to me. All I knew and all I felt was that I was done. I was no longer ambivalent, and I was ready to follow through with my decision. I stated the facts as such, and that was it. I loved him, but there was nothing I could do to help him.

The next day, two of his wonderful friends brought him home to pack his bags. We said little to each other, and then they left to take Glenn to treatment in Minnesota, where he stayed for 21 days. I think Glenn decided that he was done, too, and I slept well that night for the first time in a long time.

Glenn was going to get out of treatment the weekend after Easter. Before he returned home, he asked me to come visit, and I did want to see the place and see how he was doing, but I was reluctant to drive there by myself. I remember praying about what to do, but for some reason couldn't stop thinking of my neighbor, the one who called years ago suggesting Glenn had a drinking problem. I tried to avoid the thought, focusing instead on my prayers until the neighbor was such a distraction in my mind that I finally picked up the phone and called him. As it turned out, that neighbor was heading toward Minnesota to see their son for Easter and said I could

## Starting Over

ride with them to visit Glenn. That was definitely God helping me.

A week later, Glenn returned home. It was a blizzard that day, so instead of me driving, Glenn's brother drove from Brookings to pick him up from treatment, and I picked up Glenn from his brother's the next day. At first glance of one another, I did not greet him with open arms. There was little joy. Instead, there was apprehension, and I was looking at him closely wondering if I dare even bring him home.

Glenn was extremely weak. He was completely unwell, unsteady, and in really rough shape. Yes, he was sober, but his physical body was a basket case, which made me even more tense than I was when he was drunk. I drove us home from his brother's house, because he couldn't possibly—it would be some time before he would drive again. He had detoxed cold turkey from alcohol and all the drugs in a mere 21 days, and I believe it is a miracle he survived.

The next day, I went to work and Glenn began taking care of himself. For the next few months, he stayed at home, recuperating. If the weather was nice, he would sit on the deck and soak up the sun, letting his nerves heal a bit. He did spend quite a bit of time doing yard work, too, thinking and taking in all the sights and sounds once again. Every day, his mom would walk over to our

## Self-Portrait

house—and it was quite a long walk—just to tell him that something good was going to happen today. Just like the disease slowly crept into our life, so, too, did it leave. Even today, we continue to live and breathe, one day at a time in recovery.

> *If you treat an individual as he is, he will remain how he is. But if you treat him as if he were what he ought to be and could be, he will become what he ought to be and could be.*
> Johann Wolfgang von Goethe

🌱 🌱 🌱

But the internal dialogue did not just disappear. Even as I watched Glenn heal and even as I saw that he was safe at home, the questions continued to rattle in my mind. *Was this really going to work? Would I do something to mess this up? Were we going to make it?* There was relief, but it came with even more tension, and the eggshells I walked on while he was drinking were still on the floor, this time because I worried that I was going to somehow wreck his recovery. *Be careful here, don't do anything there.* At first, I feared relapse tremendously and just wanted so badly to be happy again. The desperation hadn't gone anywhere, it was only a new kind.

## Starting Over

I also had spent so many years consumed with thoughts of him and what he was doing, it was difficult for me to suddenly break old habits and trust that he would take care of himself. In those first couple years, Glenn had told me that, as a way of reassurance, he would call if he was ever going to be home late, and he always did. But one night, for whatever reason, he was quite late and hadn't called. Of course, my mind started spinning again. I was thinking of all the things it could be or where he could be. I still had so much doubt to remove. But in that fear, I managed to rely again on Philippians 4:8, "Finally, brothers and sisters, whatever is true, whatever is honorable, whatever is right, whatever is pure, whatever is lovely, whatever is admirable—if anything is excellent or praiseworthy—*think on these things* … and the peace of God will be with you." I thought to myself, OK, well, it was a good day, the weather was nice, it was a beautiful sunset, etc. … and by the time he got home, I was fit as a fiddle and didn't feel the need to question him at all. That gave me hope.

I had to stop putting emphasis on what Glenn was doing, what he was eating, or where he was at all times. It was very difficult for me to concentrate less on him and more on me. But after nearly 20 years of marriage, I had to learn how to trust my husband again.

Even in the alcoholism, I devoted my life to Glenn. I never gave up on our marriage, because I value marriage.

# Self-Portrait

If it were not for the choice I made to keep going, we surely would not have survived together. Even still, we had to restart that marriage—we were years behind—and sharing life together again was not immediately easy.

For years, I was essentially the only parent. I made decisions for the girls, and I made plans for our family. But with Glenn sober, he was in our lives again, and we found ourselves having to share decisions, chores, and parenting, and I really had to ease into those "new" habits. Even though I believe that when we become parents, it is our duty to care for the children as a team, I truly had to remind myself to begin including Glenn in our children's lives, telling the girls to "ask Dad" what he thought, and I was quite territorial in making that change.

The girls noticed, too. Our oldest daughter, Jen, was the one who just kind of watched her dad closely for a while—she was skeptical like me—whereas our youngest, Julie, was quick to jump on his lap with a smile. Julie has even said that she does not have a lot of memories from when Glenn was drinking, but that, too, could have been her own way of coping through it. I believe they each developed their own resiliency, but I know Glenn's drinking years affected them.

Jennifer shared with us in later years that she remembers feelings of loneliness, isolation from her dad, and the responsibility to work things out on her own. Even as a child, she felt the need to be the best she could possibly be, in hopes that might change him, and then feeling guilty when that didn't work. And then, when he did return from treatment, she felt resentment. She remembers thinking, "What are you doing here now? Who do you think you are?" She needed time to build trust, and that took awhile.

In the year prior to Glenn going to treatment, Jen was called often into the counselor's office at school, because she was failing in a lot of her classes. But at that age, she wasn't able to express what the problem was—nor was she expressing that to me—and I feel like that conveys so deeply what a child goes through in addiction. Jen was always a bright student, and by the following year she was back on the honor roll. She needed things to become secure at home before she could excel in her own life.

Even years later, Jen still feared that her dad's recovery was going to be taken away from us. She recalled moments while she was away at college and Glenn would call her. Sometimes, he would be sleepy and maybe his voice would sound a little slurred on the phone, and she would panic. *Have I lost him again?* It took years for her to build assurance that his recovery was going to stick.

I worked incredibly hard to keep the peace and then to help the girls rebuild their own trust, but I still felt regret. Glenn missed out on a lot of our kids' lives when

## Self-Portrait

he was drinking, but as it turns out, I did, too. I always accused him of not being there, but so many times, I was not mentally present either. I remember the girls would say something to me, and I would practically dismiss them because my mind was cluttered with worry about him. I have many regrets about that. It was hard. But I remember a mother saying to me once that when her kids were asleep, she would pray to God, "Take the love I gave them and help it be the love they needed," so I recited that, too. To this day, I trust it helped.

I don't remember when—the fog was only slowly lifting—but one day, amid prayer and patience and more habits of optimism, there was laughter in the house again. Whether we were laughing at the dog or the girls, I just remember actually seeing that something was funny and then feeling like I genuinely wanted to laugh. I was truly seeing and smiling, and real joy was beginning to settle into an atmosphere once stifled by years of fear and pain. Everything was lifting.

*An old Cherokee was teaching his grandson about life.*
*"A fight is going on inside me," he said to the boy. "It is a terrible fight between two wolves. One is evil—he is anger, envy, sorrow, regret, greed, arrogance, self-pity, guilt, resentment, inferiority, lies, false pride, superiority, and ego."*
*He continued, "The other is good—he is joy, peace, love, hope, serenity, humility, kindness, benevolence, empathy, generosity, truth, compassion, and faith. The same fight is going on inside you—and inside every other person, too."*
*The grandson thought about it for a minute and then asked his grandfather, "Which wolf will win?"*
*The old Cherokee replied, "The one you feed."*
(Two Wolves, unknown origin)

## Chapter Six
## Self-Portrait

It was a long road to get there, to genuinely envision a positive life for us again. I had hope when Glenn walked into treatment, but I did not regain clarity or establish a willingness to *see* the vision until I walked into Al-Anon, an anonymous community support program for people whose lives have been affected by someone else's addiction. Only there did I realize that I needed to fix me, and that could change everything for me.

I attended my first Al-Anon meeting right after Glenn returned from treatment. It was in an old apartment building, inside the group's meeting room. I sat with maybe a dozen people, and it's where I began my own healing. I'm an introvert, but I could still feel and relate to the unspoken bond among us all. Up until that

# Self-Portrait

point, I was very lonely in my suffering, feeling like I was the only one and reluctant to ever talk about it. But in that room, I heard very clearly that I was *far* from alone, and I received the affirmation I needed to not only open my heart but empathize with others as they sought their own healing. There is power in that.

Recovering from addiction is an ongoing, everlasting journey of personal growth and development. It is a new life, a second chance, and a rebirth for the addict. But seeking support from others helped me to understand that *I* needed to begin a lifelong journey of recovery, too, and that began with the realization that it was not just Glenn's responsibility to get well. I had a lot of work to do myself.

I walked into Al-Anon for the right reasons—to get help—but it was for the wrong *motive*, which was to fix Glenn. Slowly, I began to accept instead that although it was his job to work on his sobriety, it was my job to take care of me. Nobody can solve my problems—only I can do that. And I cannot solve Glenn's problems—only he can do that. So even though we *both* were getting some sanity back into our relationship, it was individualized care. I had to give him his space to heal and grow, and I had to offer that to myself, too.

I learned about this kind of self-care through a couple lectures I sat in on while Glenn was in treatment, as well

## Self-Portrait

as the relationships, curriculum, and literature I received through community support groups like Al-Anon. The resources that exist today are far more bountiful than I had years ago. But even then, it was enough to help me understand that even though I do not have the power to fix anyone, I can do *something* to fix myself, so I did. In time, I was really humbled to the fact that if I wanted to live a fulfilling life, it was not met by waiting to see if Glenn stayed sober. It was realized only when I loved and took care of me and felt peace within me. My self-portrait had little to do with Glenn and everything to do with choices I made for myself.

As Glenn worked his program one day at a time, I read my "One Day at a Time" book from Al-Anon and worked earnestly through my Twelve Step program. It really helped me along. The curriculum offered me meditations, reminders, and visualizations that not only brought about a sense of achievement, but gave me the space I needed to strengthen myself and rely on God more than ever.

When we first started the River Park treatment centers, I remember hearing about author and speaker Gert Behanna, who once told a story about her two sons. Although both her children embraced the Christian faith, one was a priest and one was an alcoholic. She did everything she could to fix her alcoholic son. She prayed and

## Self-Portrait

prayed for his sobriety until one night, God said to her, "Gert, get out of the way so I can work!" (*God is Not Dead*, Gert Behanna, 1966) This spoke to me irrevocably, and I was reminded then that I simply needed to turn my whole mess over to God.

Once I got down from my cross, admitting to myself that I was not God and that I was powerless over Glenn, an entire load was freed from my shoulders. I finally believed that a power greater than myself could restore my sanity, and what a relief! My job was simply to work on me, not to control anything else around me but simply to "get out of God's way" and allow Glenn and God to work out his sobriety.

This relief began to take over my body. Not only was it a nice change that Glenn was sober, healthier, and home for dinners at night, but I literally felt my muscles begin to relax for the first time in years. I had been so tensed up for such a long time that I didn't realize how sore my neck and back had become. It felt good to rest and relax and let those muscles sag a bit. I was feeling sane, and I was taking full, deep breaths that truly healed me with every exhale.

I also started to become so much more aware of my surroundings. Just as Glenn was being reintroduced to the beautiful sights and sounds around him, I, too, was noticing the beauty of life again. I was enjoying sunsets,

## Self-Portrait

flowers, and barking dogs. I was more alert around my kids, and church services even got better—gee, I wonder who changed? I was really joining the world again, and I'm so grateful to be here.

### FORGIVENESS

Your recovery is your own process. You do need to be well again, but how and when to start forgiving is your own journey. And it is difficult no matter how it comes.

I knew I could not change what happened between Glenn and me. I knew I could not take away the affair or the hurtful words or the many years he missed out on being a father and husband. He was sorry for them, of course, but how was I supposed to just let it be water under the bridge? As family members of addicts, we feel mad, and we want to get revenge. Even in their sobriety, we feel slighted, as if years of betrayal were just cleaned from their slate, so we waste time wanting to get even, until we realize that isn't working well and only causes both of us more pain.

Living with an addict can feel incredibly unjust, but I learned that resentment hurt me more. If I continued to harbor anger toward Glenn, it would be like me drinking poison and waiting for him to die. Resentment only

# Self-Portrait

impaired me and our children, and it surely was not fixing my years of pain. Only forgiveness could do that.

My decision to forgive Glenn first happened when he returned from California after Jen was born. He was sorry for everything he had done. But my *act* of forgiving was far more gradual. It still felt like something I had to do for my own well-being, but it was easier to do so once I wanted it for my life. And it's important to differentiate here that once I made the choice to forgive Glenn, it was done. And it is done—I hold no resentment. It is the **trust** that takes time here, as it should. I had to gain trust back after it had been absent for a long while. The journey was years long, and sometimes I think it is ongoing. We may never be fully healed, but forgiveness is so important for our own healing.

I also think people get confused that if you forgive someone, it means you have to forget whatever happened, and I do not believe that to be true. In our family programs at River Park, I assured all families that you will never forget. You may have scars from memories, but forgiveness means you can remember them without the pain. The Lord's Prayer says, "…forgive us our trespasses as we forgive those who trespass against us…" (Matthew 6:9–13) I knew it was healthier for me to forgive Glenn, and even wanting to forgive him was a huge step for me.

# Self-Portrait

As I worked on forgiveness and trust, and as I worked on myself, I watched Glenn. Just like my daughter, I cautiously sat back and thought to myself, "Let's see how this goes." One day at a time, I went to church, I put God in charge, I offered gratitude in prayer, and I immersed myself in the literature I needed to feel empowered, educated, and brave. And you know what? It went well. It got better.

*Be joyful in hope, patient in affliction,*
*faithful in prayer.*
Romans 12:12

# Chapter Seven
# It's Great to be Alive

While Glenn was still physically recovering at home, he didn't have a job for those first few months. But we wanted to spend some time together, so we tried to find affordable, fun things to do. One Friday night, we went to the store and bought groceries. It wasn't much, sure, but it was time together, and that was something we hadn't had in years. That was our treat for many weeks, and we enjoyed it. Times were really changing.

We began to not only take care of ourselves, both working our programs, but we began taking marriage seriously, bringing back the values and morals of our marriage that were once violated and lost. We communicated, asked questions, and offered guidance to one

## Self-Portrait

another in our healing. As hard as it was for me, I withheld the urge to dictate his recovery and instead offered encouragement and compassion as he regained control of his life. I knew I could not run his program, and I still cannot today. How he lives in sobriety must be his doing. No one else can do that for him, and that was freeing for both him and me.

That same understanding applied to even the trivial things in our home. I could not just throw all the booze out or ask everyone around him never to drink. Those had to be his decisions. But I could remain supportive, stay close to my own support groups, be honest in conversation with family and friends, and talk to my husband. This was real life, after all.

But real life is tough! Along with physical recovery, Glenn and I had to recover from all the financials of his addiction and treatment, too, and that was a long road for two people who hadn't communicated in years. There is more to recovery than just sobriety, which is why it is *so* important to seek support in all facets—mental, emotional, physical, and spiritual. Just like chemical dependency is a family disease, recovery from addiction is an ongoing family affair, too, that needs a lot of patience, trust, and prayer. It's a work in progress.

Shortly after Glenn came home, he got a really bad headache again. I had been worried about how we were

## It's Great to be Alive

going to deal with his headaches in his sobriety, but in this particular spell, we were up much of the night praying and trying to decide what we *could do* to help him. By the grace of God, I happened to ask him what it felt like, and my response to him was that it sounded to me like sinuses. So the next day, he went to the doctor, took an x-ray, and was sent to a specialist doctor who took one look at his records and said, "You've never had a migraine in your life. You have sinus headaches." They prescribed him Coricidin D, and he's been managing headaches ever since.

Can you believe it? This was monumental. Not only was I watching Glenn successfully work his program, we found out that all he needed for his headaches was an over-the-counter medicine. It was all so thrilling that I felt like I couldn't live this way very long either—the joy was too exhausting! We need to level off here a little bit! It was truly reassuring to watch Glenn enjoy life without the drugs. We will always be working on ourselves, but it gets better all the time, even to this day.

Less than a year after Glenn began his recovery, we established River Park. Two of Glenn's dear friends, Shanard Burke and Jack Parr, had been exploring the idea of a

## Self-Portrait

halfway house for women recovering from addiction. When they approached Glenn with their idea and asked him to help them further develop it, Glenn quickly realized that the program would only be successful if it were an addiction treatment center instead. He was also considering a different job in Kansas City, Missouri. But, oh, I prayed we didn't have to move. I was not ready for more upheaval in our lives. We all needed stability, and I was hopeful that opening a treatment center would be a good thing for Glenn and me.

We both prayed and spent many nights discussing our options, until one day, he walked in the door with a big hug to declare that we weren't going to Kansas City, and we were going to move forward with the center in Pierre. All I remember hearing was that we wouldn't be moving! I was overjoyed.

Our home in Pierre was my refuge. I spent many, many sorrowful nights comforted by the solitude and safety of our four walls. When going through a difficult time in life, sometimes a warm and familiar house is enough to ease you, and that house meant a great deal to me. I felt that a move also would have been difficult on the girls. I'm grateful that, despite any tumult in their upbringing, they had the stability of being in the same house from the time they were born until they left for college. Choosing to open River Park meant staying in

## It's Great to be Alive

Pierre and continuing to enjoy our home and friends as a family.

This was a wonderful time to be able to do something constructive together. We were making plans again! I truly enjoyed building River Park with Glenn. We were picking out bedding, furniture, and kitchenware from catalogs and figuring out costs for this and that. It was an exciting time! And I never had doubt. Not only was I excited to be a part of something that was going to help people, I didn't worry whether it would be too much for Glenn. On the contrary, it was rewarding to watch him feel valued again. He thrived in the planning and the writing and research, and the work strengthened our relationship more than we could have ever expected on our own. I still kept my day job so we could make this all work, but it was the best thing for us.

When we were developing concepts for River Park, not only did Glenn want to rely on the successful principles of Alcoholics Anonymous, it was important to me that we developed helpful and respectful programs for families of addicts. I wanted River Park to be the change I knew we needed.

When I first visited Glenn during his treatment in Minnesota, that week before he returned home, I asked the director there, "So what do I do with him now?" And he said, "I don't know." They didn't have an answer for

# Self-Portrait

me, and I was on my own again. There was no literature or counselors to guide me through even a sliver of his recovery, so that's how I knew that River Park needed to offer help for both people like Glenn and people like me. I needed to know, and I knew others did, too.

What first started as informal weekend get-togethers with a few wives and Al-Anon speakers quickly evolved into more structured family sessions that became an integral part of River Park. At these programs, families would learn about addiction and how their households had been affected. They provided intimate opportunities to iron out miscommunications, air grievances, and begin paths toward wellness. For both the addict and the family, the programs offered realization that both self-care and "the power of we" can aid recovery.

Family members also kept wanting more time to rid their hearts of the resentment and unfairness they had been feeling for so long as well as time to grow and learn. When spouses would walk around River Park, so many of them would yearn for the care they saw their loved one getting. The addicted person was being fed well, sleeping well, attending meaningful lectures—all while not working, not paying bills, not taking care of their kids, and not fulfilling the responsibilities that *the spouse* was left with at home by themselves. And then, when the addicted person came home from treatment, the attention was

# It's Great to be Alive

*still* on them, leaving the family member feeling entirely ignored. It was also hard for them to give up the control they had while their loved one was gone—I struggled with that, too, relinquishing my control to make room for Glenn's input. It's tough giving up being boss, but these grievances only validated the importance of family programs and having some kind of support group to lean on and empathize with during this sensitive time. I also believe that it's not good to send a recovering addict home to an angry or withdrawn family. Everyone needs help, and our family programs became a great safety net for the whole family.

It is so important to me still today that I help families understand how the addict feels in this disease, too. They do not want to be put in this position, either—to have their entire life uprooted, their character tested, their faith and strength challenged. Both the addict and their loved ones are faced with their own kind of adversity and recovery. In addiction, no one is superior. Everyone is hurting, and I'm incredibly grateful that we were able to offer family programs at River Park to at least introduce the care and dialogue families deserve to begin their own kind of rehabilitation. Just like an addict is entitled to respect and dignity, the family members of an addict deserve to regain their self-worth, too. It might take a lifetime to get there, and you will need to take lifelong

## Self-Portrait

precautions, but there *is* help. There is always help, empathy, and understanding if you seek it.

River Park thrived for nearly twenty-five years, helping families not only in South Dakota, but across the nation. And it was such an overwhelming, powerful experience for Glenn and me. When we first opened the treatment centers, we thought it would help so many people, and now we look back and worry it didn't make a dent! But on the other hand, opening River Park—and sharing our story—is like throwing a pebble in the water. We might not see where the pebble lands, but we do see ripples out there, in the children, grandchildren, and great-grandchildren who might benefit from our efforts. You might start a ripple, too, and that gives us hope.

Years have passed. Glenn and I have worked on ourselves, which has also helped the other—a win-win. I never feared relapse in the later years, but it could've happened, or I could have even been in his shoes, God forbid. But I know now that we would have been dealing with a disease and would have sought the right help to move forward. There have been new challenges, of course. We both had broken bones, Glenn had stage four cancer and now has diabetes. There are and will still be more ups and downs for us, I'm sure. But we've been married nearly seventy years, and through it all, it just keeps getting better. It truly is great to be alive.

## It's Great to Be Alive

At River Park, and still today as I fulfill God's calling on my life, I remind people that I always have a choice. I can choose to stay in the past or grow in the future. I can choose to react or act. I can choose to struggle making people into what I want or work at making *me* into what I want. And, I can choose to work on myself knowing I can change. It is a lifetime effort, **but I do have choices.**

*God grant me the serenity
to accept the things I cannot change,
courage to change the things I can,
and the wisdom to know the difference.*

## Part II

# Reflections

When an addict or the loved one of an addict has arrived at a new physical or emotional low in their chemical dependency, it can be referred to as rock bottom. But what rock bottom looks like is different for everyone. It might be an event or circumstance that motivated them to change, or it might come from feelings of desperation that there is little to nothing left. It is at these times that most family interventions take place.

For me, I endured Glenn's drinking for far too long. I literally sat there for years, watching the situation get worse. My patience and resiliency is not only uncommon here, but it was not safe, and it could have cost Glenn his life. Even though we must

# Self-Portrait

*wait for an addict's readiness to change, people can die in that time. If you choose not to get help or intervene, it could be too late.*

*Glenn has always said, "You can lead a horse to water, and you can't make them drink, but it might make them thirsty." Just like that call from my neighbor helped me to recognize Glenn's drinking problem, an intervention might wake your loved one up to what is happening and leverage their thoughts. As family members, we also are in a unique position to know an addict's patterns of behavior well, which means we might be able to find a narrow window that catches them at the right moment and provokes awareness of the detrimental situation. Both an addict and a family member can be blinded by addiction, and sometimes an intervention is the first time the problem is even brought to light.*

*In times of intervention, plan ahead, and bring in a trained professional who can help both the addict and the family/friend/boss/child/parent ease into the conversation. Do not treat the intervention as a confrontation motivated only by hurt and anger. That will go nowhere. Instead, talk about how the negative behaviors affect you. It takes a good salesman, which is why you need to involve experts. But if an intervention is done with care and concern, it can be cathartic not only for family members, but also helpful for the addict, as they see a group of people who care about their wellbeing.*

*Above all, if you are feeling unsafe, do not wait any longer to get help for you or your family. Regardless of your*

## Reflections

*circumstance, you are a person who is somebody. You are important, you deserve to live, and you must take care of yourself first to be able to help anyone else.*

*When the addict gets into treatment, and even long after he or she has returned, give yourself permission to take care of yourself by seeking ongoing support, education, and rehabilitation. As far as I was concerned, Al-Anon and the Twelve Steps saved my sanity. Thankfully, there are far more resources available today for family members of addicts, which means there are many ways to regain your strength. Look through resources listed at the back of this book, and find what works for you. You can also participate in individual therapy with a mental health professional or an addictions professional who is knowledgeable about working with family members of addicts.*

*Community support and community resources are vital for strength and serenity. I only began to feel calm and confident when I sought guidance, and I believe a changed culture will not come until even more people come forward for support. Addicts and family members of addicts have an opportunity to become advocates for change, and I believe the only way we can make a dent is by eliminating the stigma and shame, educating our communities, and helping society to recognize addiction as a medical condition. Just like diabetes, cancer, or heart disease, addiction is life-threatening if left untreated. We have a long way to go, but even you being here means that you have become a part of that awareness.*

# Self-Portrait

*As your loved one continues their recovery, promote positive communication that is supportive instead of accusatory. Encourage all positive activities that your loved one is engaged in, such as attending AA meetings, seeking sponsorship, or finding new hobbies. And as you engage, ask them what they need for support. Talk to them as you would an esteemed colleague—people tend to respond well to respect—and avoid drudging up the past or expectations for the future. Live in the present moment, focus on today, and take it one day at a time.*

*In adulthood, we cannot take anything for granted. We can always be improving, learning, and growing. Even though it can be difficult to muster energy in times of adversity, those are absolutely the circumstances under which to stand up for yourself, get educated, and take action. Engage in literature, connect with a counselor or someone you trust, communicate bravely with the addict, and pray like heck. We have today—all we have is now—and today is a good day to look at yourself, embrace your worth, and begin a portrait of you.*

# Resources

Consult the following programs to begin taking care of yourself and your family:

### AVERA

At the Avera Addiction Care Center, family members are encouraged to participate in the Avera Addiction Family Program while their loved one is in treatment. During the program, participants learn how to establish new communication skills and healthier relationships with their loved one. Addiction services use criteria for admission, continued service, and discharge developed by the American Society of Addiction Medicine (ASAM).

Avera Health is a collaborating member of the Hazelden Betty Ford Patient Care Network. Visit Avera.org/addictioncare to learn more or call 605-504-2222.

### FACE IT TOGETHER

Face It TOGETHER is a nonprofit organization established in 2009 that provides effective, science-based peer coaching for people living with addiction, including loved ones

# Self-Portrait

of those with the disease. This community believes that people impacted by addiction, including their families, deserve the same dignity and respect as anyone else affected by a serious illness. They offer coaching centers in Colorado, South Dakota, North Dakota, and Minnesota, with clients in more than fourteen states. Visit wefaceittogether.org, call or text 855-539-9375, or seek out mutual support groups at addiction.com or smartrecovery.org.

### HELPLINE CENTER

The Helpline Center began serving the Sioux Empire community in 1974. The mission of the Helpline Center is making lives better by giving support, offering hope and creating connections all day, every day. The center fulfills its mission through the following core service areas: 211 helpline, volunteer connections, and suicide crisis support. Dial 211 to be connected to the resources you need for help and for hope. Visit www.helplinecenter.org for more information.

### IT'S GREAT TO BE ALIVE

For more information about River Park and Glenn's book and television series, visit ItsGreatToBeAliveBook.com.